the POWER of PERSONAL VISION

7 KEYS TO DISCOVERING YOUR PERSONAL VISION

Rodney D. Robertson

Impact|Publishing

Impacting your world with inspiration™

BATON ROUGE, LA

the**POWER**of
PERSONAL VISION

Copyright © 2011 by Rodney D. Robertson

ISBN 13: 978-0-578-07043-8
Printed in the United States of America.

Published by:
Impact Publishing, LLC
PO Box 74610
Baton Rouge, LA 70874

Cover/Interior Design by:
www.r2design.com

CONTENTS

PERSONAL NOTE

You are embarking on an awesome journey for your life. *The Power of Personal Vision* was written for individuals like you and I who are tired of merely existing and going through the motions. We want our lives to count. We want to live life on purpose passionately.

You may ask, "How do I do that?" I'm glad you asked. You can live a life on purpose passionately by discovering your personal vision for your life. Now, this is not going to be one of those books where you need a PhD, dictionary, and encyclopedia to understand the principles you will discover as you continue to read. I am keeping it simple and practical so that you can begin right where you are in your world.

PERSONAL NOTE

Vision is not just for churches, organizations, and businesses. Vision is also vital for your personal life and the lasting impact you were created to leave on this earth. When I die, I want the world to know that Rodney D. Robertson was here. Likewise, you should also desire to leave a lasting mark on this world that cannot be erased. The memory of you and I should be blessed because of the lives we have touched by tapping into our personal visions.

Starting right now, I want you to make a decision that you are going to discover the *Power of Personal Vision* and live life on purpose passionately. There is more to life than what you are experiencing. Get ready to discover your personal vision for your life.

Excited about your future,
Rodney D. Robertson

KEY #1

Discover Your Purpose

Purpose is the reason why you were born.
It answers the question "Why am I here?"

—R.D. Robertson

Discover
Your Purpose

E veryone has a purpose. The fact that you were born and came to earth denotes that you have a purpose and God has BIG plans for your life. Whether you are the CEO of a thriving corporation or the president of the PTA club; you have purpose. You were created to be a leader in your area of expertise and to do great things that will leave a lasting impact on the world.

You are an original. You are God's masterpiece. There will never be another YOU. Your style, personality, skills, gifts and talents are unique. You have been set apart for a specific purpose that will enhance the lives of others.

KEY #1 Discover Your Purpose

Now that raises a question, what is purpose? Purpose is the reason why you were born. It answers the question "Why am I here?" Purpose reveals to you what the Creator had in mind when he created you.

I remember when I didn't know my purpose and how I experienced feeling unfulfilled and a deep sense of void in my life. I had social connections but no divine connection. I didn't know my purpose. I was moving through life, but I wasn't living life on purpose. I was simply going through the motions.

Connect with the Creator...

I often made the mistake of asking people what they thought I was born to do, and the only thing I got was a lot of opinions and more confusion. What I learned from that was people cannot answer the "Why" question for you. **Only the Creator can answer the reason why you were born here on the earth.**

Therefore, if you and I are going to discover purpose; it's going to come through having an intimate relationship with the Creator. Why the Creator you say? The Creator is the one who created you and he knows the intricate details of your life. He knows why you are wired the way you are wired.

He knows your weaknesses, strengths, fears, dreams, giftings and skills. He knows you inside and out. In fact, he is passionate about his relationship with you (Exodus 34:14 NLT). He is so in to you. He wants to see you succeed in life and be the leader in your area of gifting.

Since He knows you the best, why not build an intimate relationship with the person who knows why you were created. If I wanted to know why a computer was created, I wouldn't consult the salesman. I would consult the creator or inventor because he could tell me specifically what he had in mind when he created the computer.

The salesman can tell me the benefits of the computer but he cannot tell me why it was created. Likewise, people

KEY #1 Discover Your Purpose

cannot tell you your purpose. You and I must go to God, the Creator. And that's exactly what I did. I went to the Creator (the source) and not people (resource) and my divine purpose was revealed to me.

Once I discovered purpose, it was like I had awakened from a long winter's nap. I had been in hibernation. Purpose was my alarm clock that woke me up to live life on purpose. It was time to be present in my own life. I no longer had to go through the motions or the routine of life. I could now live life on purpose.

Knowing purpose gave me clarity of why I was created the way I was created. I was able to understand me better and how I was wired. Through purpose, I gained an appreciation for my uniqueness and realized that it was ok to be ME. I did not have to be anyone else but ME.

You have purpose and the Creator wants you to know your purpose. He wants your life to have meaning and a sense of focused direction. He wants to awaken you from hibernation so that you can live life on purpose and not as an experiment. However, it does require your cooperation. You must make the connection. You must enter into a relationship with him so that he can reveal to you your divine purpose.

After you discover purpose, you will become more aware of the good things God has already equipped you with to fulfill your divine assignment and personal vision. You have everything you need to carry out your personal vision and purpose in life. In fact, your discovery of purpose will attract the resources and the key people who are instrumental in helping you to fulfill purpose and realize your personal vision.

You have purpose. *God created you to succeed and you are only going to succeed when you discover purpose and function in your area of gifting.* Know today that you are a success going somewhere to happen. God has a purpose for your life, a place for you to be and a people for you to connect with.

KEY #1 Discover Your Purpose

Tap into your passion...

After connecting with God who is the source of purpose and vision, tap into your passion. What are you passionate about? What do you deeply care about? What do you love doing that even if no one paid you, you would continue to do it? What would you live for? What would you die for?

Tapping into your passion is one of the paths that I believe will connect you with the purpose for which God created you. Though passion alone is not a 100% guarantee of discovering purpose, it will lead you into the right direction of what you were born to do. Passion is the energizer of successful people who live life on purpose. It is the fuel for the pursuit of your purpose and doing the thing you love to do.

Identify your gifts...

Once you tap into your passion, do not stop there. Why, because passion can only take you so far. You will need to identify your gifts. When I talk about identifying your gifts, ask yourself, "What am I good at? What do I do well? What are my strengths? What sets me apart from the crowd?"

I love KFC's slogan. KFC says, "We do chicken Right®." KFC makes it known that they do chicken right. It is their specialty. Doing chicken right sets them apart from their competitors. With that being said, what do you do right? What are you so good at that others find it difficult to do?

When you are gifted in an area, it comes natural for you. There is no struggle or strain. It is so natural that it is easy. You just flow because it is your gift or strength. When you operate in your gift, it sets you apart and lifts you above the rest. **Your success is found in doing something you love and doing it well.**

Focus on your gifts or strengths instead of focusing on your weaknesses. Why, because focusing on your weaknesses will never make you strong or successful. Be aware of your weaknesses or limitations but focus on your strengths. **Wherever your focus goes, your life will follow.** You will experience what you give your attention to whether it is negative or positive.

Discover • Develop • Demonstrate

Average is average and no one pays attention to average or ordinary. Therefore, after you have discovered your gifts it is important that you move to the next stage of your discovery. Your gift must be developed. Develop your strengths. Sharpen your skills. Practice. Practice. Practice.

Your gift will make room for you and bring you before great people if it is developed. No one pays for average. If you are going to rise above the crowd, then you must be intentional about your personal growth and strength development. Perfect practice gives birth to great performances. **Practice in private and shine in public.** Work on your strength. Fine tune your gift. Take it to the next dimension.

Now that you have discovered your gift and developed it, it is time to demonstrate. Meaning, you must put your gift to work. How do you put your gift to work you say? You put it to work by using your gift to provide service and add value to others. You were created to meet a specific need on the earth in an area of gifting that is unique to you. Use your gift. Demonstrate. Display your strengths. Shine in public.

Vision Reminders:

- God created you with purpose.
- Purpose answers the question "Why am I here?"
- Purpose gives your life meaning.
- Life without purpose is a nightmare.
- The Creator is the source of purpose.
- Tap into your passion. What are you passionate about? What do you deeply care about? What do you love doing that even if no one paid you, you would continue to do it? What would you live for? What would you die for?
- Identify your gifts. Answer the questions, "What do I do right? What am I good at? What do I do well? What are my strengths? What sets me apart from the crowd?"
- Your success is found in doing what you love and doing it well.
- Develop your gift.
- Practice in private and shine in public.
- Demonstrate your gift.
- Use your gift by providing service and adding value to others.

Reflection: In a quiet place, look within and answer the following questions.

Why am I here?

My purpose is... _____

_____

_____

_____

_____

_____

_____

_____

_____

What am I passionate about?

_____

_____

_____

KEY #1 Discover Your Purpose

_____

_____

_____

_____

_____

_____

What are my gifts or talents?

_____

_____

_____

_____

_____

_____

_____

_____

_____

KEY #2

Get Inspired

Our chief want is someone who will inspire us to be what we know we could be.

—Ralph Waldo Emerson

Get Inspired

*It is the Spirit of God that made me [which has
stirred me up], and the breath of the Almighty that
gives me life [which inspires me].*

—Job 33:4 AMP

n Latin, inspire means to breathe upon or into.
According to *Webster's New World Dictionary &
Thesaurus*, inspire means to inhale, to stimulate as to
some creative effort, to motivate as by divine influence, and
to arouse a thought or feeling in someone.

These definitions are right on it. In order for one to
get inspired, he must allow God to breathe in him. The

breath of God not only comes to give us life; it also comes to inspire us. When God breathes in us, he motivates and prompts us to creative activity. *The breath of God arouses new creative thinking within our minds. The breath of God arouses new feelings within our hearts that cause us to connect to his heart and the plans he has for our lives.*

The breath of God is powerful. **Whenever God breathes into us, we are filled with his life and those things that are lifeless in our lives will receive a second wind and be revived.** This is very important to personal vision because life can throw some curve balls that can knock the life out of your hopes, dreams, and plans. However, your divine dreams, thoughts, visions, goals, and plans are going to be resuscitated by the breath of God. The breath of God is going to awaken those things that lie dormant within you. Why, because God is looking for a return on your life from the investment he made in you. He wants to use your life to make an eternal difference in your world.

When one is just ambitious, he is the only benefactor of his efforts. However, when one is God inspired, not only does he benefit, but the people in his life and community also benefit and are changed because of the breath of God he has received.

Now, the question may be, "How do I get inspired?" I'm glad you asked. Ask God. Ask him to breathe into you so that the creative potential within you can be stirred up. I know that sounds simple, but because it's so simple many people have over looked this simple principle and not received the breath of God. Ask God to breathe into you and expect him to do it. Why, because everyone who asks receives (Matthew 7:8).

God wants to inspire you. He wants to breathe into you so that you can be internally motivated to accomplish the things you have been created to do. Get inspired. Inhale the breath of God. Allow God to stimulate you internally so that you can tap into your passion and live life on purpose. *Get inspired!*

Vision Reminders:

- In order to be inspired, one must allow God to breathe in him.
- When God breathes in us, he motivates and prompts us to creativity.
- Inspiration from God arouses new creative thinking in our minds and new feelings within our hearts that cause us to connect with His plans and purpose.
- Whenever God breathes into us, we are filled with his life and those things that are lifeless in our lives will receive a second wind and be revived.
- Ask God to breath into you.
- Everyone who asks receives.

KEY #3

Get a Vision

Vision looks inwards and becomes duty. Vision looks outwards and becomes aspiration. Vision looks upwards and becomes faith.

—Stephen S. Wise

Get a Vision

If people can't see what God is doing,
they stumble all over themselves;
but when they attend to what he reveals,
they are most blessed.

—Proverbs 29:18 The Message (MSG)

Within all of us, there lies a divine vision and purpose for our lives that requires us to go back to the Creator and receive answers about our lives and our life-callings. Only the Creator can answer the "Why" question for our existence and direct us in the plain path for our lives.

KEY #3 Get a Vision

When I say get a vision for your life, I am not talking about something you dreamed up last night after eating a big bowl of spaghetti and meatballs. Get a vision for your life is a challenge to you to go to God and tap into the divine deposit that was placed in your heart before your mama knew your daddy.

Once you tap into your personal vision for your life, you will become a greater asset in any corporate vision i.e., family, church, non-profit, or organization. Once you receive a vision for your life, it is going to affect all areas of your life. Getting a vision for your life will impact your relationships, business, family, and finances. Getting a vision for your life will supply you with the fuel you need to live an authentic life on purpose.

What is a vision...

In order to experience the benefits of a thing, one must have a working definition of what it is so that the power of understanding can be released and then he can manifest the destiny that God has predetermined for him. Without a vision or revelation of what God has in mind for our lives, you and I would merely exist. You and I must have a clear revelation of what God has in mind for our existence on the earth. With that being said, I want to share with you my personal definition of vision.

Vision is a revelation of what God has in mind for the future. To make it personal, vision is a revelation of what God has in mind for your (my) future. It is a view of what can be and it requires faith and action to bring it to reality. I like the word revelation because it suggests that something is being unveiled. It was always there, but now it is being revealed or brought to light.

What God has in mind for your future is being revealed to you through vision. God does not want you to live your life as an experiment—spending countless of hours, days, and even years hitting and missing. He wants you to know why you were born and how you are

25

KEY #3 Get a Vision

destined to make an eternal difference in your world and leave a mark that cannot be erased. God wants you to see yourself in the future and know that there is more available for your life. *You can be more, have more, do more and experience more.* There is more to life than what you are experiencing. Getting a vision or revelation for your life is a good step in the direction of experiencing God's BEST for your life.

At the beginning of this chapter, we opened with a quote from the Message Bible. It said, "If people can't see what God is doing, they stumble all over themselves; but when they attend to what he reveals, they are most blessed." This is right on it. When people cannot see what God is doing in reference to their lives and future; they stumble all over themselves, miss opportunities, and wander aimlessly in life. However, if they can see what God is doing, they are most blessed or empowered to prosper and succeed in life, relationships, business, ministry, etc.

God wants you to know his vision for your life and the plans that he has in mind for you to positively influence the lives of others. He does not want you to keep spinning your wheels and going nowhere. He wants you to get a vision for your life and follow the plan he has outlined for you. In fact, God says, "*I know what I'm doing. I have it all planned out—plans to take care of you, not abandon you, plans to give you the future you hope for*" (Jeremiah 29:11 MSG).

Vision comes from...

Now that you have a working definition of what vision is, let us talk about where vision comes from. Vision comes from purpose and purpose is given from God to every individual. God has created every one of us with a purpose and placed in our hearts vision for our lives.

Purpose is given to help you and I understand and know what we were born to accomplish in our lifetime.

KEY #3 Get a Vision

Vision is given to us so that we can see what we were born to accomplish in our lifetime. **Purpose gives us the power to know why we were born and vision gives us the power to see why we were born.** They both go hand in hand and without them we would only exist. Purpose supplies us with the inside information we need to see the future (vision) that God has planned for us. Without vision and purpose, our lives will lack meaning and significance and life will be merely an experiment.

The purpose of God for our lives is eternal. *The plans of the LORD stand firm forever, the purposes of his heart through all generations* (Psalm 33:11 NIV). In addition, *Isaiah 14:24 NIV says, "The LORD Almighty has sworn, 'Surely as I have planned, so it will be, and as I have purposed, so it will stand.'"* Therefore, the purpose of God is permanent and prevails. It prevails over your imperfections, past, social and economical status. The purpose of God for our lives stands forever.

Look in your heart...

The first place to discover your purpose and vision is to look to God. After looking to God, then look in your heart. *He has made everything beautiful in its time. He also has planted eternity in men's hearts and minds [a divinely implanted sense of a purpose working through the ages which nothing under the sun but God alone can satisfy.]* (Ecclesiastes 3:11 AMP)

In the heart of every individual, God has planted eternity, a divine sense of purpose that can only be satisfied by him. A piece of eternity has been placed in your heart so that you can know and see from eternity's perspective what you were born to accomplish in your lifetime.

God, the Creator, the Master of the universe has planted vision, a sense of purpose, and the desire of eternity in your heart. Wow! The answer for your existence, your career choice, the vision for your life, is in your heart. *Your heart holds the revelation of what God has in mind for*

29

KEY #3 Get a Vision

your future. Your purpose and vision is not without you, but it is WITHIN you.

I learned through personal experience that vision is revealed and functions in the heart. I can remember so many times looking to things and people for the purpose of my existence. However, I only ended up with more disappointment and frustration. I made many bad choices and took wrong paths because I failed to look into my heart. I ignored the desire of eternity, the deep call of purpose in my heart and I wandered aimlessly in life empty and frustrated. I was frustrated because I knew in my heart that I was created for something greater than the life I was living. I wanted more for my life!

It was when I looked into my heart that I got the vision (revelation) for my life. Revelation is hidden knowledge that is brought to light or made known. The knowledge was there all the time but it was hidden to my mind. Now that it is revealed, my mind has an understanding of what my heart knew all the time—my purpose and personal vision.

Look in your heart. Tap into your passion and follow your God-given vision. To my college students, choose a major that complements your passion. Do not make a professional career choice based solely upon the "money". If you do what you love, the money will follow. *The money, resources, and people will show up when you are found doing the thing you were born to do.*

I know many friends and relatives who chose careers for the money. Once they did it for a while, they lost interest and no longer wanted to do the career they chose based solely upon the money. They hated going to work because what they were doing was not in their hearts anymore. They followed the status quo and not their passion. Your passion is the thing you deeply love. It is the thing that most incites you and prompts you to take action. It is the thing you love doing and would do it even if no one paid you. Tapping into your passion will point you in the right direction of your purpose.

Do not listen to the strange voices outside and the people who are not you. You know the ones who say, "If I were you." Guess what? They are not you and everyone's purpose and vision is unique and personal. Look into your heart. Discover the purpose and vision God has planted in your heart.

Vision Reminders:

- Only the Creator can answer the "Why" question for your existence.
- Vision requires a relationship with God.
- Vision is a revelation of what God has in mind for your future.
- God doesn't want you to live your life as an experiment.
- Vision emanates from purpose.
- Purpose gives us the power to know why we were born and vision gives us the power to see why we were born.
- The purpose of God for our lives is eternal.
- In the heart of every individual, God has planted eternity, a divine sense of purpose that can only be satisfied by him.
- Your heart holds the revelation of what God has in mind for your future.

KEY #4

Write it Down

If you want to be remembered well after you pass away, either write things worth reading or do things worth writing.

—Ben Franklin

Write it Down

Then the LORD answered me and said:
"Write the vision and make it plain on tablets,
that he may run who reads it."
—**Habakkuk 2:2 NKJV**

W rite the vision down. Now that you have received your vision for your life, write it down. Do not trust your memory. Write it down and make it plain. Get a pen and some paper and write down what God has revealed to you in your heart about your future. I know it sounds simple, but many people skip this step and do not experience the power of writing down what God has shown them in their hearts.

Writing down your vision is your initial act of faith. It is you putting in words what has been revealed to you in your heart. Even if you do not quite understand it all, write it down. Even if you cannot see how your vision is going to come to pass, write it down anyway. Your assignment is to believe what God has revealed to you through vision and write it down. The how and the when is God's department. Just write it down!

Get a plan...

Writing the vision down involves getting a plan. If you and I are going to prosper and succeed in life, we are going to need a plan. Why—because if you fail to plan then you plan to fail. Writing down your vision gives you a tangible target to aim for. It is writing down what you want to happen. Your personal vision must be taken from your heart and transferred onto paper.

A man's heart plans his way, but the LORD directs his steps (Proverbs 16:9). Now, if you do not have a plan, how can God direct your steps? In the words of Joan of Arc, "Act and God will act." You are not waiting on God to move. God is waiting on you to bust a move.

Another word for plan is "prepare." You must prepare yourself for the appointed course that has been destined for your life. **Opportunities come to prepared people.** Prepared people are not getting ready. They are ready and ready to do what they were born to do. They are prepared; their skills are sharpened and they are equipped to get the job done.

Write down your vision. Put a plan in motion. Set goals to reach your vision. Review your plan and make changes when necessary. Be prepared.

Make it plain…

When writing your vision down, it is important to *make it plain*. The Scripture says that we should make it plain on tablets (paper) so that he may run who reads it. To every purpose and vision, there is connected to it a people. This people, I will call a support team. A support team is a select group of people who believes in you, supports you, challenges you, prays for you, looks out for your best interest, and speaks the truth to you in love.

Every visionary leader needs a support team. It is imperative to make it plain so that the runners (your support team) can read it and run with it. Your vision should be so clear that a person can read it and catch your vision in his imagination and heart and carry it out. **Vision is caught and not taught; however, if the vision is not clear it cannot be caught.**

Make it plain. With your words, paint a clear picture of what God has revealed to you through vision. Keep it simple. No fluff. Communicate clearly. Share with the runners (your support team) what God has revealed in your heart so that they can carry out your vision. Know that God did not call you to do it by yourself. **Yes, without a**

vision the people will perish; however, without a people the vision will perish also.

Right relationships with people are vital to the success of your vision becoming reality. As John Maxwell once said, "One is too small of a number to achieve greatness." In order to achieve the great things that have been assigned to your life, you will need the assistance of a support team. So again, make it plain so that the runners (your support team) can read it and carry it out. Make it plain!

Vision Reminders:

- Writing down your vision is your initial act of faith.

- Writing the vision down involves getting a plan.

- Set goals to reach your vision.

- Review your plan and make changes when necessary.

- Make it plain. With your words, paint a clear picture of what God has revealed to you through vision.

- Without a vision, the people will perish. Without a people, the vision will perish.

KEY #5

Find Your Own Company

*Associate with men of good quality
if you esteem your own reputation;
for it is better to be alone
than in bad company.*

—George Washington

Find Your Own Company

And being let go, they went to their own company,
and reported all that the chief priests
and elders had said unto them.

—Act 4:23

Our success in life, relationships, business, and ministry depends upon the people we surround ourselves with. I call them your "*own company*." Now when I say your "own company," I am not speaking of people who look like you, dress like you, talk like you, and always tell you yes to whatever you ask.

KEY #5 Find Your Own Company

When I say be found among your own company, I am saying be found among people who love you enough to tell you the truth in love regardless of your title, position, possessions or power. In fact, faithful are the wounds of a friend (Proverbs 27:6). The wounds from a friend can be trusted. **You can rely on a real friend to hurt you, but only with the truth.**

Your own company is a select group of people who celebrate you and not just tolerate you. Being found among your own company is a good place. It is a place where your differences and uniqueness is respected and not looked down upon. Finding your own company means surrounding yourself with people who complement your gifts and talents and not compete with them. You are accepted and no one is trying to change you into their image of you.

When you are found among your own company, your character is developed and your skills are sharpened. Just as iron sharpens iron, friends sharpen the minds of each

46

other (Proverbs 27:17 CEV). Your skills are sharpened, your thinking is elevated, your perspective is broadened, and your faith is strengthened after being in the presence of your own company. In fact, your life is better after being in the presence of your own company.

Surround yourself with competent people who are going in the same direction you are going in. Choose your friends, your own company carefully. Why, because *a mirror reflects a man's face, but what he is really like is shown by the kind of friends he chooses* (Proverbs 27:19 TLB). The company of people that surrounds you speaks volume about who you are as a person. In fact, I can predict your future by the company you keep. **Your own company is either propelling you into purpose or rushing you into ruin.**

Bad company does corrupt good character; however, you and I have a choice. We are not able to choose our relatives, but we can choose the people we call friends. If you do not like the direction your friends are taking you,

KEY #5 Find Your Own Company

change it. Let them know that your life has purpose and
that you can no longer take the route they are going in.
They may not understand this change of direction, but
they will respect you for being honest and telling them
the truth.

So right where you are in life, begin to evaluate your
relationships, the people you call friends, and the direction
your life is going. If your life is not moving in the direction
of your purpose with your present company of friends,
then change your company. Know that you deserve to
have good, healthy, and productive relationships. Choose
your own company wisely.

Vision Reminders:

- Your success in life, relationships, business, and ministry depends upon the people you surround yourself with.
- Faithful are the wounds of a friend.
- You can rely on a real friend to hurt you, but only with the truth.
- Your own company is a select group of people who celebrate you and not just tolerate you.
- Surround yourself with people who complement your gifts and not compete with them.
- The company of people that surrounds you speaks volume about who you are as a person.

KEY #6

Stay F.O.C.U.S.

*People with goals succeed
because they know where they're going.*

—Earl Nightingale

Stay F.O.C.U.S.

Let your eyes look right on [with fixed purpose],
and let your gaze be straight before you.

—Proverbs 4:25 AMP

I n order to talk about staying focus, we must first discuss habits. What is a habit? It is something you do so often that it becomes automatic or second nature. It's a habit. You have been doing it for so long that it is easy. In fact, some habits can be performed without even thinking about it.

Developing good habits take time and a consistent effort on your part. It is not going to happen overnight. Why,

KEY #6 Stay F.O.C.U.S.

because you have to be honest and consider how long you have been practicing the bad or negative habit. However, the good news is that you can start today by developing good habits especially in the area of staying focus.

Before you and I can develop good habits, we must first take an assessment of the bad habits that have been sabotaging our success and holding us back in our relationships, health, business, and personal lives. Why, because you cannot change what you're unwilling to confront. Identifying your bad habits will give you the edge you need to develop good habits and replace bad habits.

If you keep doing what you've always done, you'll keep getting what you've always gotten. Change is required. Before your relationships, health, business, and personal life change, you must change. Nothing will change in your life until you change. You and I must be the agents of change in our own lives.

Developing good habits is essential for staying focus. How do you change bad habits? Good question. I'm glad you asked. Here are three ways to change bad habits and develop good habits.

1. Identify your bad habits

Identifying your bad habits require honesty and transparency. You must be willing to see yourself and things the way they are. Being in self-denial is not going to help you. It will be a hindrance to your progress. *Every action has a consequence and the actions you take today are building your future for tomorrow.* Therefore, look closely at the habits or negative behaviors that are holding you back and sabotaging your success.

2. Replace your bad habits with good habits

It's not enough to stop a bad habit if you don't replace it with a good habit. For every bad habit, there is an opposite or good habit for it. Replacing your bad habit with a good habit is paramount to your development of good habits. It's not enough to stop doing the wrong thing. You must start doing the right thing. Learn better. Do better.

3. Implement a P.O.A. (Plan of Action)

Now that you have identified the bad habits and found their opposite, it is time to implement a plan of action. Start where you are and take on one bad habit at a time. Take action. In this stage, you will be required to be consistent. Why, because consistency is the key to victory. As you consistently take action, your momentum to replace bad habits with good habits will increase and you will raise your quality of life.

We are what we repeatedly do.
Excellence, then, is not an act, but a habit.
—Aristotle

Focus Breakers...

In order to be successful in life, one has to stay focus. You and I must be ruthless with distractions. As we grow and progress in life, there will be some "life pop-ups" that will try to break our focus. If you'll be honest, some of the things that came up weren't always "emergencies" or "important." At first glance, they appeared BIGGER than life. However, when you took a second look, you could see that it really wasn't that BIG or that SERIOUS.

I call these interruptions *focus breakers*. Focus breakers are attention thieves that come to interrupt your focus, hinder your progress, and divert your attention away from your purpose. They may come in the form of people, things, or circumstances. No matter what form *focus breakers* come in; their objective is to steal your peace, attention, time, energy, and ultimately your success.

KEY #6 Stay F.O.C.U.S.

What are the focus breakers in your life and how are they affecting you?

_____

_____

_____

_____

_____

_____

_____

_____

_____

_____

Why people fail...

People fail in life because of broken focus. It's not because they didn't have a plan; they allowed the *focus breakers* to break their focus. When one's focus is broken, frustration builds up, goals are not pursued, and life assignments are unfulfilled. Total focus is the secret of every success whether it is in relationships, business, or personal life.

Whatever you focus on or give your attention to will magnify in your life. Wherever your focus goes your life will follow. For example, if you focus on not having enough, then you will see and experience more of not having enough. If you focus on what doesn't work instead of what works, you will see and experience more of what doesn't work. Moreover, if you focus on what you can't do instead of what you can do, you will see and experience more of what you can't do. *Change your focus change your life.*

Your life will move in the direction of your focus. Therefore, it is vital that you avoid wasting your time on things, people, and circumstances that do not help you in maximizing your potential and fulfilling your purpose.

No more broken focus. Your mind is an employee. Give it an assignment and tell it what to think about and focus on. I like what Earl Nightingale said about the mind. He said, "*The human mind is just like fertile farm land. It does not care what you plant, but it will return whatever you plant.*" Whatever you plant in the mind it will produce in your life. The mind doesn't care what you plant, but it will produce whatever you plant. Therefore, it is imperative that we cultivate right thinking in our minds. Our thinking (thoughts) gives birth to our decisions. Our decisions give birth to our actions. Our actions give birth to our habits and our habits give birth to our character. And it all started with our thinking—what we repeatedly think about.

Stay F.O.C.U.S.

Stay F.O.C.U.S. (Fixed on Creating Ultimate Success). It is important that you and I stay fixed on creating ultimate success. Success is not by chance. Success is a choice and it is our responsibility. We are where we are in life because of the decisions we have made.

Nothing in life just happens. Even faith, if it doesn't have corresponding actions; it is dead, useless. You and I must be intentional about our success whether it is in relationships, business, career, finances, or personal life.

When I say be fixed on creating ultimate success, I am speaking of having a laser-like focus. In order to live life on purpose, maximize potential, and dominate in your area of gifting, you are going to need a laser-like focus. How do you develop a laser-like focus? Good question. Here are 6 ways to develop a laser-like focus.

1. **Be specific**. Get clear on what you want. Focus your attention on what you want instead of what you don't want. Visualize your goals. Experience the positive feelings associated with having what you desire. Know what you have to do to achieve or obtain your desired goals. Keep your vision before you.

2. **Confront inner conflicts**. Identify the lies you are telling yourself why you can't have what you want. Discover what's stopping you from experiencing ultimate success in relationships, business, finances or personal life. Find out the root cause for you sabotaging your own success.

3. **Take action**. It's not enough to visualize or believe. You must take action. You must take

61

corresponding action. Your action or movement should correspond to your personal vision so that you are moving closer to your desired goal. Your actions should complement your vision and the positive feelings you have about what you desire.

4. **Connect with a mentor**. Success leaves clues. Model the experts who are successful. A mentor can save you a lot of time, pain, and money by gleaning from his wisdom, mistakes, and experiences.

5. **Be consistent**. Consistency is the key to success in every area of life. Let your thinking and actions align to your personal vision.

6. **Be relentless**. Don't settle for anything that is less than God's best for your life. Remove quitting from your vocabulary. Winning is your only option.

Vision Reminders:

- Identify bad habits that hinder your focus.
- Replace bad habits with good habits.
- Implement a P.O.A. (Plan of Action).
- Identify focus breakers.
- Whatever you focus on will magnify in your life.
- Your life will move in the direction of your focus.
- Our thinking (thoughts) gives birth to our decisions. Our decisions give birth to our actions. Our actions give birth to our habits and our habits give birth to our character.
- Stay F.O.C.U.S. (Fixed On Creating Ultimate Success)

Take Action

Vision without action is a daydream.
Action without vision is a nightmare.

—Japanese Proverb

Take Action

If you wait for perfect conditions,
you will never get anything done.
—Ecclesiastes 11:4 NLT

o many times in life, we miss divine opportunities to grow, expand, and advance because we sit by waiting on perfect conditions. **There are no perfect conditions.** In fact, life is not perfect and some seasons of life can be down right challenging. However, if we are to see the manifestation of our personal visions; we must be willing to take action.

KEY #7 Take Action

Waiting for perfect conditions will result in getting nothing done. We say things like "When I get more money…When the children leave the house…I will do it tomorrow…I am too young or I am too old and my time has passed." As a result of statements like these, we end up doing nothing and going no where in life. These are mere excuses we use to sabotage our own progress and success in life.

You may never have enough money. Your children may leave and come back for some reason or another. Tomorrow is not promise and all you have is the gift of now. Oh yea, the age thing is not a factor. If you are young, use your strength and agility to your advantage. If you are older, your time has not passed. You have a wisdom that is priceless and is much needed by the younger generation. Whether young or old, male or female, we must take responsibility for our actions and move in the direction of our destinies.

A dream comes with...

A dream comes with much business and painful effort (Eccl. 5:3 AMP). There is a price to pay when acting on what you believe. The vision will come with painful efforts and heartaches. It is going to cost you your time, energy, resources, and some relationships that are not adding to your life. However, if you have made a decision to pay the price in order for your vision to come to pass, God will grant you the grace to take a licking and keep on ticking.

We must participate in the manifestation of the vision for our lives. **Dreams and visions become reality when we take action.** We have to do the plan that we have written down and made plain. It is not enough to believe in your vision if you are not willing to act upon what you believe. Faith is active and it is now. It requires you to act like what God said to you is true. It requires corresponding action—action that is in harmony with your faith. Faith by itself is dead or useless, if it does not have corresponding actions.

KEY #7 Take Action

It is insanity to keep doing the same thing over and over and expecting different results. The insanity about the situation is that what you are doing does not work; however, you keep doing it over and over again. In order to have something that you have never had, you must do something that you have never done before.

Decisions, decisions...

Change begins with a decision. The decisions you make are changing your life for better or worse. Your decisions are either helping you to manifest your vision or to forfeit your God-given vision. Your life is moving in the direction of your decisions. **Decisions decide your destiny.** In fact, the Bible says that God has set before us life and death, blessing and cursing and then he gives us the answer to the multiple choice question. He says, "Choose life that you and your seed may live." Choose life. Make wise decisions because there is a people (seed) connected to your decision. It is BIGGER than you.

I know making decisions are not comfortable at times; however, you cannot be afraid to make decisions. Even if you decided I'm not going to make a decision, you have still made a decision. The decision you made is to do nothing about the situation.

One of the keys to making good decisions is having good information. You cannot make a good decision based upon assumptions, hunches, or the opinions of unqualified people. Decisions made upon such things will result in unfavorable outcomes. *Good decisions are made when you have good information.*

Sometimes in order to get good information, you may have to leave your comfort zone and seek out wise counsel. Why, because there is safety and victory in the abundance of counselors (Proverbs 24:6 AMP). What you don't know you can find it in the wisdom and experience of another. God fixed it so that we need one another. Everyone has something to offer that's of value. **People are your greatest resource.** Someone knows something that you need to know. Their knowledge and experience could save you from unnecessary pain and wasted time that you will never get back. *Good decisions are made when you have good information.*

Decide today to take action. And not just any kind of action, but action that corresponds with your personal vision and purpose. Be intentional and proactive about your personal success in relationships, business, finances, etc. Take action. Add action to your faith. Believing is not enough. You must ACT! Go for it!

Vision Reminders:

- There are no perfect conditions.
- Waiting for perfect conditions will result in getting nothing done.
- There is a price to pay when acting on what you believe.
- Dreams and visions become reality when we take action.
- Decisions decide your destiny.
- The decisions you make are changing your life for the better or worse.
- Good decisions are made when you have good information.
- People are your greatest resource.

ABOUT THE AUTHOR

For over ten years, this dynamic, multigifted life changer has been equipping people to discover destiny, maximize potential and to use their lives to make an eternal difference in the world. He is a highly respected preacher, songwriter, relationship coach, mentor and a speaker who is known for "*keeping it real.*"

Rodney D. Robertson is the founder and CEO of New Life Christian Center in Baton Rouge, Louisiana. He is also an entrepreneur, publisher, and author. He is the author of best sellers such as *Free to Be Me!, How*

ABOUT THE AUTHOR

to Keep a Good Man, and *You are Not the Mistake.* He is married to his beautiful wife, LaKeida Robertson. They reside in Louisiana.

CONTACT INFORMATION

Whether you received *The Power of Personal Vision* as a gift, borrowed it from a friend or purchased it yourself, we're glad you read it. We hope that you will share this book and its message with your family and friends.

If you're interested in writing the author, wish to receive free newsletters, would like information about his speaking engagements or would like to invite Rodney to speak at an event you are hosting, please visit his website or send your written correspondence to the address listed below:

Rodney D. Robertson

PO Box 74610

BATON ROUGE, LA 70874

www.rodneyrobertson.org

CONTACT INFORMATION

Stay Connected with Rodney:

Become a friend of Rodney on

www.facebook.com/rodney.d.robertson

Follow Rodney on

www.twitter.com/rodneyrobertson

OTHER BOOKS BY RODNEY D. ROBERTSON

Order your copy of any of the following titles today at

www.rodneyrobertson.org

Volume Discount Available

Contact us at:

Impact Publishing, LLC

Attn: Publisher

PO Box 74610

Baton Rouge, LA 70874

EMAIL: impactpublishing@ymail.com

HOW TO KEEP A GOOD MAN

ISBN: 9780615186986

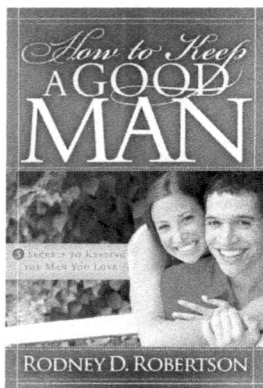

A good man is hard to find. In this day and time, a good man is a rare commodity. Inside this best seller, you will discover the secrets to keeping a good man without the help of tricks, schemes, games, and love potions.

You will discover love solutions that will reveal what a good man wants and how you can keep him. If you're already married, your love skills will be sharpened. If you're a lady in waiting, you will be equipped with meaningful insights for the good man that is on the way. *Get ready to enjoy more of life, love, and a lasting connection with your good man.*

Available online at:

www.amazon.com

www.rodneyrobertson.org

YOU ARE NOT THE MISTAKE!

ISBN: 9780615261959

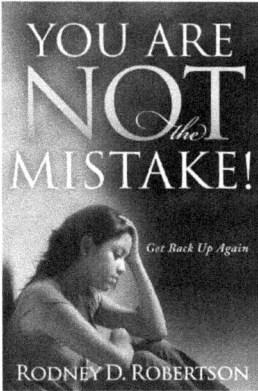

You are not the mistake you made! Inside this life changing book, Rodney will show you how to make a comeback from the place where you've fallen. Through his message of hope and restoration, you will find out that God still loves you, he stands ready to forgive you and you can get up again.

Inside *You are Not the Mistake*, you will learn things like:

- How to find life after the mistake,
- How to forget it and move on,
- How to worship your way to wholeness,
- How to get free from the guilt of the past and so MUCH MORE.

It is your time to get up and walk in your destiny. It doesn't matter if you have fallen one time or 101 times.

OTHER BOOKS...

You aren't what you did. Though a just man falls seven times, he will arise again (Proverbs 24:16). Get ready to receive God's forgiveness, healing, the power to forgive yourself, and the strength to walk in victory every day. **You are Not the Mistake!**

Available online at:

www.amazon.com

www.rodneyrobertson.org

Also available from Impact Publishing, LLC

HOW TO RECOGNIZE A GOOD MAN

ISBN: 9780578022062

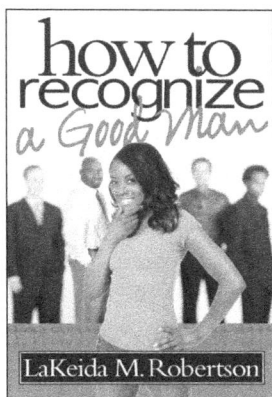

Inside *How to Recognize a GOOD Man*, LaKeida will share with you her experiences combined with divine wisdom on how to recognize a good man, the value of knowing who you are, and the power of knowing if the man you're considering is a part of your destiny. Get ready to be empowered! Get ready to be enlightened! There is a GOOD man that God has prepared for you and LaKeida wants to help you to recognize him.

Available online at:

www.rodneyrobertson.org

FREE RESOURCES
For Relationships

To get your free relationship resources from Rodney D. Robertson, simply visit our site at:

www.rodneyrobertson.org

Get ready to take your friendships and relationships to the next dimension!

www.ingramcontent.com/pod-product-compliance
Lightning Source LLC
Chambersburg PA
CBHW060135050426
42448CB00010B/2138